GOD
GIVES ALL
THINGS AT THE
PROPER TIME

Susan Essary

WESTBOW
PRESS®
A DIVISION OF THOMAS NELSON
& ZONDERVAN

WestBow Press
A Division of Thomas Nelson & Zondervan
1663 Liberty Drive
Bloomington, IN 47403
www.westbowpress.com
1 (866) 928-1240

ISBN: 978-1-5127-7794-9 (sc)

WestBow Press rev. date: 02/28/2017

My mother was a constant encouragement in every phase
of the completion of this book.
Mom, thank you for believing in me. May I, by God's hand,
be a blessing to you.

My challenge as a writer is this:
How do I come up with a refreshing arrangement of words?
The truth is I don't; He does.
Each life is a masterpiece of His own arrangement of irises.

Foot note. (irises) The pigment of the eye.

CONTENTS

PREFACE

These are some of the moments of my life, past and present. He moves within me the desire to write them down and so I do. This is not your typical storybook in which you will read one story from beginning to end, it is a book of poems and memoirs; The writer's experiences as lived. My life (as was yours) was well thought out in the mind of God. The pages you hold are some of my experiences of His thoughts, that He has shared with me, lived out through a gift of life.

The book contains many stories about a girl named Heather, my daughter. The story of her and her pony are intermingled throughout my book of memoirs.

This book was to have originally been a child's book but, as I began to write, it proved to be more for an adult audience.

The book also includes some Bible Scripture.

LIFE IS A FRAGILE GIFT FROM GOD!

When I was in my youth I wanted to be a writer. It did not happen in my youth. I wrote a few thoughts down, but not much came to mind. So the desire quietly lingered on.

A little more into my mid life years, thoughts began to come to me. We are not omniscient (having infinite awareness, understanding, and insight). Life must be slowly unfolded to each one of us. The teachings of my Lord and Savior now come to me, saying "Be kind to one another". So may I encourage you at this time to think "Let's be kind to one another". Don't go and tear someone else's package open for them. Because like myself, the gift needs to be slowly opened by someone who knows how not to break what's inside.

He knew and He waited
Until
I clearly understood what I was saying no to!
Before
He drew the line in the sand
And as I took his hand I stepped over the line.

GOD GIVES ALL THINGS
AT THE PROPER TIME

The spring of 1999 was the year my husband and I decided to begin our search for the horse that our daughter, Heather, had long been waiting for. We were told that the County fair would be a good place to start. The day we started off to the fair just happened to be a beautiful, bright blue skied, sunny day. I was unaware of the fact that the sunny day would be what set the stage to a bitter sweet adventure in our lives. My daughter and I were destined to meet a horse named Sonny! At that time in our lives we were attending a quaint little church, tucked away in the beautiful landscape of North Central Ohio. I was fairly new to the church, so the people at the church were only familiar faces to me. Heather and I had never been to see the horses at the fair. As we wandered down through the aisle ways, we must have had the appearance of being lost. I was approached by a nice, polite man who said, "I believe I have seen you at the church I attend". I said "Oh yes, I know your face". He asked what we were there for. I told him we were there looking for a very gentle, child safe horse. He said "We are looking for the same thing that you are looking for! However, what you're looking for has been loaned to us". Through a good Christian friendship they were able to free lease a child safe horse. As he continued the conversation, he told us of how he had tried his best to persuade the owner of the horse to sell this wonderful horse to him. Then with gentle kindness he took my daughter and I to see the horse.

As we approached the horse the man told us of how at times, he had almost pleaded with the horse's owner to sell the horse to him for his own daughter. But, the owner of the horse would only loan the horse to them. We listened to him as he could not say enough good about the horse. The horse's name was Sonny Dee Bret. The horse stood there so nice and quiet as if he had been working hard at the fair. He stood 15.2 hands high and had a sweet handsome face with a heart shaped star on his forehead. The Lord placed it there when he gave Sonny his personality. He was a lot of horse and he was long enough to put three kids on his back. Sonny Dee Bret is line bred to Sonny Dee Bar. Line breeding is when one horse is used at the start of both male and female breeding line. You breed two horse's that have one same horse in their blood line.

I walked away sad. There stood just what I wanted, but it was unattainable. I walked away speaking to God from within. "Father, other people are blessed with good things, why can't I find a horse like that? That's what I really need!"

Looking back, I know my Heavenly Father was watching me and might have said something like this; "My child only knows disappointment now. But later in life she will see my patience and why there is a place and a time for everything".

As I walked away, I did not know that a little more time had to pass before God would send that same horse (Sonny Dee Bret) to our farm. If He had given the horse to us at that time, I would have missed out on one of the biggest blessings of my life.

As it happened we were unable to find a good horse, but we were told about a pony named Pudge. This pony was said to have a good track record so we went to take a look. The first time I saw Pudge, I thought what a pathetic looking creature. My first impression was wrong. God knew just what He was doing. He was going to bless my heart in a big way. He knew his child had no clue of what to do with a horse let alone an old 4-H pony named Pudge. Pudge was an old 4-H pony; he had been through four generations of children and knew just what to do, so we were told. Pudge knew just what to do all right! He knew we did not know what we were doing so he thought he could get away with being a little stinker. He was old and wise and God had painted an ornery looking swish on the side of his face for a reason. Well, when we got to their farm, they had Pudge saddled up and ready for Heather to try out. Their neighbors had a round pen that was available for us to use so we walked down the road over to their house. The family that owned Pudge seemed to be honest (help your neighbor) kind of people. They were very kind to us. Heather was a bit timid around new people as are a lot of children at the age of seven. I think she did not know what to think of the situation. This was the moment she had been waiting for and it was now taking place. As we walked down the road some of the near by neighbors were outside using guns for target practice; But Pudge walked confidently down the road. He was a brave little pony. When we got to the round pen, Heather was hesitant to climb aboard, but she did. Heather asked him to walk, and then she asked for a little bit more. She wanted him to pick up the pace. Well, wouldn't you know that this wonderful little pony bucked! Right then, in Heather's mind, this was a signal to get in the car and go home. Heather's riding instructor was there with us and with a little quick thinking on her part she spoke a few words of encouragement and helped Heather work though the situation.

I cannot put into words the joy Pudge brought to my family and me. We had him for six years and during that time we almost lost him twice. After many tears and prayers he would recover and take his girl for more rides. I do not want to know what it is like not to have him. It will be hard to let go of one of the biggest blessings of my daughter's childhood. God loves a mother's heart.

They say when God closes a door, He always opens a window. Perhaps when He, at just the right time closes that door, the horse with a heart shaped star on his face will still be looking in the window.

These first few pages were written close to two years before Pudgy went to sleep. There was a third time we almost lost Pudge. I believe that is when the Lord put it into my heart to write these first few pages. I had never intended to write a book. It still amazes me how these first few pages were thought out two years before Pudge went to sleep. I did not know these writings were to be the first three pages to this book. I just sat down one day and wrote the first part of this story in Heather's blue folder, lay the folder aside and never gave a thought to preserving it. Heather had a blue folder filled with paper that she used when as a child she played. Sometimes Heather and her friends would use it to play school or store or what ever they needed it for at the time. The blue folder had a lot of pictures of Pudge drawn in it. On the outside of it she had Pudge's name written all over it. Sonny was lucky enough to have his name written once on the front. It is amazing to me that this folder survived all those years of careless child's play. It had been shuffled around to all sorts of places but somehow it would keep appearing throughout the years.

About a year after Pudge was buried, it was put into my heart to write about what I believe to be an outstanding answer to my prayer. That was the motivation given to me to look for and find the blue folder. I needed the first few pages for this book.

THE FIRST STEP!

THE FIRST DAY we had Pudge (our new pony) it quickly became evident how unprepared we were to receive him. A friend had given us a list of items we would need for the new arrival. We purchased everything on the list, so we thought we were ready! We had a barn, a field, a water bucket and pony food. When Pudge was delivered, we went to put him in his new stall and that's when we discovered that we needed a gate so that he would stay inside of his stall. Pudgy's previous owners chuckled a bit and said, "Well, I guess you could just tie him up until your husband gets home, and then hopefully, he can make a gate for the stall." Poor Pudge, not only could we not keep him in his stall, neither could we let him out to graze, for the weeds in the field were taller than he was.

I'LL BE WAITING FOR YOU!

HEATHER ATTENDED THE public school system at the end of her second grade school year. She quickly made friends. It was easy for her to make friends because she just seemed to naturally like everyone! I could take Heather just about anywhere and shortly thereafter she would be having a good time with someone! Heather had many friends in her class as well as throughout the school; she even made friends outside of her own grade. That school year I volunteered as a teachers assistant in her class. I was surprised that she had so many friends and they all knew that she was supposed to be getting a horse. Even the school secretary knew it.

When we moved to central Ohio we made sure that the house we chose would have a place for a horse. Heather's time schedule for the purchase of a horse was just a little sooner than ours, although she never gave up hope. At the beginning of her third grade school year her friends began to wonder about it. Shortly after school had begun she finally got her wish. She got a pudgy little pony. Of course she could not wait to tell everyone at school and guess what! No one believed her, and that made Heather feel awful. One day she asked me if I would stand out by the driveway with Pudge and wait for the bus to bring her home from school. So the next day, I was out there with Pudge. As the bus approached our house Heather had all the kids on the bus looking out the windows ready to see that this pony was real.

After Heather was off the bus and as she came over and took pudge from me, I asked her, what did the kids on the bus have to say? She told me she did not know. They were all speechless.

OUCH!

I T DIDN'T TAKE me too long after Pudge came to our house to understand that horses are thinking creatures. One summer day I took Pudge out to walk him around our front yard. A neighbor came walking by and stopped to say Hi. As I held Pudge by his lead rope while talking to the neighbor I was not paying much attention to the little pony. He did it so slowly that I never even noticed, until my foot was a little under pressure. Pudge had ever so quietly moved his foot over, and placed his hoof right on top of my foot!

I moved my foot out from under his and didn't think much of it. I did not know that this was just one of his sneaky little tricks he liked to play on new people. As time went on I began to notice that occasionally when Pudge would be standing by someone he did not know, without it being noticed, he would quietly move his foot over on top of that person's foot. One time he did this at the Pony Club Heather was a member of, and the little stinker broke one of the advisers big toe!

TO HEAR HEATHER CALL

I CAN STILL hear the voice of Heather. Crystal clear it could be heard throughout the four levels of our home. Heather would bring Pudge (her pony) in through the garage and up to the kitchen door and holler "Mom". No matter how often or what kind of mess I had gotten myself involved in, the echo of Heather's voice in the garage would send me moving quickly to the kitchen door. Her voice was always filled with love and honor. She was bringing her most precious friend to see her mother. Her voice told me that I could be counted on to always receive them as a blessing from above. Sometimes I would receive this blessing many times a day. Hot summer days would bring Heather to the kitchen door. She and Pudge would come riding in because Heather would be thirsty in need of a drink, and Pudge would take that time to catch his breath. What a pair they were. They seemed so like-minded, as if they knew they were well taken care of, and they enjoyed it! They were two cuties! What a wonderful friendship that had been developed through time spent together in those childhood years. It's strange how few those years are and how fast they go by, but the time spent within those years seems eternal. What a blessing from God. Do you think this childhood state of mind is a gift from God? A gifted glance of what eternity is like? He gives this gift of childhood to each person whom he has created and no one is cheated out of this gift. How clever to start out life with eternity in mind. Even though it may be hard to let go of the past, without knowing the truth, these precious words of a time gone by could be just that... time and words that just disappear. But the truth is, God our Father holds the past, present, and the future in his hands. They are not of time to him.

Now, getting back to the kitchen door, the first of many visits, Heather hollered out "Mom," I have a surprise for you! When I got to the door I was surprised. Heather had brought Pudge into the garage while both cars were parked inside. I almost scolded her, but she was so bursting with happiness I could not. To reward Pudge for being such a polite visitor, I searched the cabinets for a treat. This quickly became a routine. She and Pudge would come into the garage and she would holler "Mom", and as she could hear me getting closer, she would always say gladly in a loud happy voice, "there is someone here to see you." When I would get to the door, Pudge would be standing there. He knew Mom would find some kind of treat and bring it out to him. What a blessing! It's not all moms that receive such visitors. I discovered that ponies like to eat much more that just grass and oats. They like dried cranberries, bananas, raisins, dried apricots, carrots, strawberries, grapes, apples, pears and even prunes. Pudge really got to like mom's kitchen and it was never hard to get him to come in through the garage.

I believe our little pony is in heaven now. I tell Heather even though these are wonderful fond memories, it hurts! But that's okay, because some day (God willing) she's going to live right next to me in heaven, and then she and Pudge will come and visit me. And maybe, from the back door I'll hear Heather call out in a loud happy voice "Mom, there is someone here to see you!"

Nose to Nose.

Mark 10:14 But when Jesus saw what was happening he was very much displeased with his disciples and said to them, "Let the children come to me, for the Kingdom of God belongs to such as they. Don't send them away!"

Snow Ride

PUDGES FIRST WINTER WITH US

A S THE SPRING had taught us new things about ponies, so did the winter snows. The first big snowfall Heather and I bundled up in our warm winter clothing and went out to play with Pudge. Heather had never ridden a pony in the snow before and did not quite know what to expect. We saddled him up and even though she had been riding him all summer long, she was quiet and it was as if she was riding him again for the first time. She rode him to the dogs' pen, came back and then she was done. Heather's pony ride in the snow looked like a lot of fun, so I thought I would try a pony ride in the snow myself. I had my thick snow pants on and I was really quite surprised. Up until then, I just could not understand how these animals could stay warm. That little pony was like a warm furnace! I could feel the heat right through my thick snow pants.

Another thing that tickled Heather was the first time Pudge came in from the snow with great big snow caps on his hooves. He came up to the barn walking kind of funny. We thought something must be wrong; it looked like he was trying to walk with high heels on. When we got him in his stall we found that he did have heels on, and those heels were made of ice. I got the hoof pick and pulled them off and Pudge seemed to really appreciate it. I told Heather those ice caps looked like they could really make his feet sore. So from then on when Pudge came in with those ice caps, I would pull them off and he always seemed to be glad of it.

It was also this first winter Pudge expressed to me the great need a pony has for food during the cold winter months. It was quite often that I was greeted by Pudge with a loud whinny. As soon as he saw me, he would throw up his head and whinny. In the winter it sounded almost blood curdling. I told my husband and the girls that it sounded like Pudge was saying "Saaaave me". He needed food and he needed it right now! I am hoping that when I get to heaven I will be greeted with the beautiful sound of Pudge's whinny. I wonder how the different creatures in heaven sound. The Bible tells us that there are horses in heaven. Can you imagine the majestic sound of all the horses calling out to the Lord!

I'LL JUST DO IT MYSELF

DURING THE WINTER months Pudge looked like a furry red bear. But even though he looked so well dressed in his fur coat, as he got older he had a hard time with the cold. I think he wasn't getting enough intake of hay. It seemed like he was eating enough but a lot of ABC (already been chewed) hay could be found lying about. Older animals require a lot more time and care. I used to get big bags of alfalfa cubes for Pudge to help keep him warm. The cubes were too hard for him to eat so every day throughout the winter I would fill up his bowl with cubes and let them soak in water for a couple of hours. When Pudge saw that pan being served, he would have a mini celebration and jump right in. He would eat them as fast as he could. He seemed to be just starving at times.

One time during the winter I forgot to dress Pudge in his little blue coat, his winter blanket. It got very cold that night. When I got out to the stall that next morning, Pudge was whinnying and anxiously moving about. I always kept his blanket draped over the side of his stall. I was surprised to see his coat lying on the ground. It was the only time he had ever messed with his coat. Of course, I fed him and put his coat on right away. As I stood there I wondered, might he have pulled it off the wall just to try to help himself get warmer. I laughed to myself and thought as I envisioned him thinking, "Well, if she is not going to come out here and put my coat on for me, I'll just do it myself"!

OOPS! I ATE TOO MUCH!

PUDGE'S FIRST WINTER with us was a learning experience. When the veterinarian had been out to see him in the fall she told me Pudge was to have free choice hay because that is what keeps horses warm. So that winter Pudge had all the hay he wanted. He became so furry that we really did not notice how pudgy he was getting. When spring came and the weather was nice enough to ride in, Heather and I headed out to the barn to get the little pony saddled up. Boy, did Heather have a good laugh while she was putting the saddle on! She discovered that there was more than just fur underneath. When I heard her good, hardy laugh I took a look! His girth could not have been put on even with a girth extender. His little youth saddle looked like it was going to pop right off his back. I told Heather he had so much padding from his thick fur coat that maybe she really didn't need a saddle. So off came the saddle and away they went.

We did not have the money for a new girth, so Heather just kind of worked things out on her own. She wanted to ride, so that spring she became really good at bareback riding. It was about a month or so and she had Pudgy back into shape but even though his girth fit him again she found it more convenient to just tie a rope to his halter, then jump on and go! She even taught herself to jump bare back. I think more times than I want to acknowledge it, I would be better off if God does not provide something I think I need, I should just wait and see what comes our way.

During the time we had Pudge it seemed that there were just never enough extra funds to buy a trailer. Heather wanted so badly to take him places. She wanted to go to the Fair and all the 4-H practices; she wanted to go to horse shows and the USPC (United State's Pony Club) of which she was a member. She had the perfect kids pony! I could never figure out why God did not provide a trailer. But there is that old saying, (Father knows best)! Heather's riding instructor was kind enough to trailer Pudge for us when she could. One time it had worked out that her instructor was entered in a horse show and she offered to give Pudge a ride if Heather wanted to go. The instructor would be leaving in the morning and planned on staying there the whole day. Heather was in school that day so the woman had asked me to have Pudge ready. Now I have waited out at the end of the driveway many times with Holly and Heather for the school bus, but this time I found myself standing out there with a pony, waiting for the pony bus. Actually, Pudge was going to be schooled that day, which it is called by the English horsemen. He truly was a new addition to the family.

THE LAST RIDE

PUDGE WAS OLD and as time went by I began to understand his sufferings, even though he hid them so well. He hid them so well we did not noticed all that was wrong, since he always acted like he was tough as nails. The last week he spent on this earth, he ran his heart out for Heather. Heather's childhood friend from out of state came to spend a week with us. This was Heather's horse buddy. Their friendship began through the love of horses and they dreamed of one day riding horses together. The two girls became friends at the end of their first grade school year. They had become friends about three months before we moved to another state. I wasn't sure why, but in my heart I had this feeling of also wanting their dream to come true. What were the chances of that? It seemed like something to think and dream about; but to really come true? God showed me that He was the one that gave the desire, because of no special planning of my own, it came true. Although this did not come without cost to me. It took a lot of time, work and money, all of which I was lacked. I am not the type of person to take responsibly too lightly. I guess what I am trying to say is, I had a large homestead, two young children, a husband who was away from home, five animals, five acres to mow, and a swimming pool. I kept things clean, everyone was well fed and I had absolutely no living relative in the state in which we lived. I had once heard something I'll never forget: "Do not reckon the cost of an action when the results are worthy". We cannot be of great use to others without self giving.

That year of 2004, my husband was working out of state. The two friends had made plans for a summer visit at our house, so I found myself making a trip to pick Heather's friend up. The trip was about a six and a half hour drive one way. I had to get a sitter for all the animals, which was not easy.

The girls were full of excitement. They wanted to make the most of their long awaited visit, but to my disappointment, their vision of the visit was the extreme opposite of mine. I thought they would be out there with the horses so much that I would hardly have to take care of them. Wrong! They expected me to be a short order cook. They thought they should be able to eat whatever and whenever they wanted. They only rode and played with the horses. They thought that the only obligation they had to the horses was to be just pure fun. That week I found myself identifying with the life of Cinderella. I was always five steps behind all of their messes. They were a whole lot faster than me. I kept trying to convince myself that I should be happy they were not just sitting in front of the television. But couldn't they sit for just one hour and watch a video?

One day I had to go to the store and the girls did not want to go so I told them that my oldest daughter Holly was going to stay home and watch them; I wouldn't be gone long and that they were not allowed to ride the horses while I was gone. Well on my return home, as I neared the house, I wondered why the car that was a little bit ahead of me had slowed down and almost stopped at the top of the hill. When I reached the top of the hill, I found out why. Just on the side of the road hiding behind some of the trees stood Pudge and Sonny. Sitting a top of them were Heather and her friend. I told myself do not get all stressed out; just leave it alone and just make them go to the store next time.

Yes, they found all kinds of things to do with the horses. One day I went downstairs and found Pudge in the house watching television with Heather and her friend. Heather had always wanted Pudge to see who Mr. Ed was. (For those of you who may not know who Mr. Ed is, Mr. Ed is a horse featured on one of the old television shows.) Do you think I am kidding? I have pictures!

Another thing Heather had planned for herself and her friend was to make use of the old garden. One of Heather's favorite past times was playing in the dirt. She liked it even more when it was mixed with water. All of Heather's friends knew, if you played at Heather's house, make sure to bring clothes you can get dirty in for Heather spends most of her time outside. She can always find something to do out there.

I had fixed a small garden by the barn. I only used it for a couple of years. When I decided to quit using it, Heather was more than happy to make use of it. There was a hole dug in the garden from soil that was used somewhere else. This hole was a Godsend to Heather. She made use of the hole by making a giant mud puddle. If she got bored playing in the mud hole alone, she would go and get good old Pudge. After she wore Pudge out by making him jump the water hole as many times as he could, it would be the dogs turn. I remember Heather telling her friend about the old garden. Heather was so happy because she was going to have someone to play with in the muddy garden for a whole week.

Heather was also glad to have a good rain. Usually when that happened the lower field would have standing water. She would jump on Pudges bare back and off they would go. Pudge would have the water flying as he charged on through, and boy, that would satisfy Heather's spirit. Could anything else be as much fun?! I think Pudge liked it as much as Heather did. When they were done they both would be dripping wet and plastered in mud.

Oh, every time I think of Heather and Pudge, it is like re-reading a favored story book written by my favorite and the greatest author of all time (God).

Well, I started out to tell you how Pudge had become injured. We took Heather's friend back on Friday. We returned home on Saturday. Heather had ridden Pudge several times a day everyday that week and Pudge had worked hard. I had been too busy to notice, but later on seeing the pictures taken of Pudge that week, you could see his age and he was just worn out. I don't even think he cared; old Pudge would have carried Heather until every last drop of his energy was gone. God bless my baby! He had a God given desire to give it his all.

The Field.

Now, when we returned on Saturday, Heather took Pudge out again. She took him about a mile down the road where there was a creek near the end of the street. Heather and Pudge had jumped it many times before but this time they did not quite make it over. I don't know if it was the mud that had gotten too deep or the creek that had gotten too wide, or was Pudge just too worn out, but, for the first time ever Pudge fell. He fell right on top of Heather. (Thank you Jesus for being there!) Heather was bareback and barefoot. In the summer, I never could get her to ride Pudge with shoes on her feet.

When Pudge got to his feet and Heather had gotten up, she realized her foot had gotten hurt. Her leg had gotten caught under his pudgy belly! Pudge was pretty sure footed; I figured there was some kind of good reason for his fall. Heather said Pudge seemed like he wasn't able to carry her back home. Heather told Pudge she couldn't walk and there wasn't anyone near enough to help them. The only one that knew of their trouble was Jesus. Heather said it was as if Pudge understood. I did not know it then, but I know it now that he was hurt more than we will ever know. The brave little pony loved his friend, because in his condition he faithfully carried her all the way home (God bless Pudge; he was hurt and couldn't tell us). When they got back to the house, they headed straight for the garage. Heather hollered through the kitchen door "Mom hurry we need you". I went out to see what was wrong. I looked at Pudge; I didn't see anything wrong with him. Heather was complaining about her foot, so I told her just to put Pudge away and stay off her feet. Later that night Heather went out to feed Pudge and Sonny. When she came in she said that Pudge didn't seem to want his food. I thought that was strange, but that week and the two trips had worn me out, so I just let it pass, I'd see him in the morning.

Next is a cherished writing I was honored to read at my fathers funeral service November 11, 2014 at 11:00 A.M..

In loving memory of
Waymon Essary

Titled
Touched by the Son

TOUCHED BY THE SON!

WALKING DOWN THE road on a bright but cold sunny day, a feeling came over me. I remembered what it felt like to have my father get me ready to go out into the cold. This feeling took me quite by surprise. I am now 46 (56) years old and I don't think I've given a thought to it over the years. I believe I was thanking my heavenly Father for the warm sun at the time. I know it was Him that had brought it to my attention. I remember so clearly my dad putting my coat on. It was a wonderful feeling, a feeling of protection. He always made sure things were done just right. I was well taken care of as a child. When the coat was zipped up, I would stand there nice and quiet, because that is what he had taught me to do. All I knew at the time was just to stand there, and have that feeling of having nothing to do but stand there and be taken care of. It felt good! Worry free!

As I walked down the road with the sun on my face, I could feel the warmth coming through my coat. That was my heavenly Father putting his warm coat of sunshine on me, and all that I had to do was just smile. And now that's a good memory too. It is, as if now I know that whenever the time comes for me to leave this world, my heavenly Father has already gotten my traveling coat on and I'll be ready to go.

A SEASON PASSES AWAY

NOW THAT I have taken the time to make record of *Touched By The Son*, something else has been brought to my attention. It was the day in which my little Pudgy went to sleep. That particular summer had a very slow start. That June was just cold for the most part. It was so cold, that up until that day in June, Heather needed to wear her heavy blue Adidis sweatshirt very often.

The weather put before us a gloomy day which became appropriate for what was about to be set before us. Pudge's time had come; he was to go to sleep and wake no more. Right before Pudge was about to pass, he leaped up towards the sky and at that moment there was an opening in the clouds and the sun came out and shone down on him. As Pudge returned to the earth, the clouds quickly covered the sun. I think my Heavenly Father has told me that He had clothed Pudge in warm sunshine and ever so lovingly had taken him to safety. Shortly after he had fallen asleep it started to rain. I think God was trying to tell us He could feel our grief. I do not believe anyone can properly put grief into words, but I know that Pudgy has no pain now. I don't know how he could have been so brave. He just stood there like a brave little solider. Heather bravely stood right by his side. I told Heather "a true friend will not leave you". We could not let him die alone. Heather put on her blue hoodie and snuggled up to Pudge. As I looked upon Heather as she sat on the ground in the rain next to Pudge my heart was overwhelmed with sorrow. What could I do, I have loved animals all my life and I fully understood how she felt. I had quite a few good dogs, but this little Pony Pudge touched my heart in a different way. It might have been because of the way he carried my much loved child. When we first got him, I did not know that a pony could be your friend. I did not know that outside of a dog other animals had personalities too and could be communicated with as such. I guess Pudge had shown me that there is a reason for each animal.

Well, I hated to leave Heather and Pudge out there like that in the rain, but I knew Pudge had to be buried that day. I could barely think or even walk at the time; there is something very special about a child's first pet and the first departure. I headed for the house to look in the phone book for someone who could dig a grave for Pudge. My neighbor saw Heather out there in the rain and was kind enough to bring Heather an umbrella. While I was in the house I found and old bed cover that had belonged to Heather's paternal grandmother and took it out there to cover up Pudge. Heather never knew her paternal grandparents. They had been gone many, many years before Heather"s birth. I am sure her grandma would be quite thankful to know that something of hers was used, (for the granddaughter she never knew) in one of her greatest times of need. After I had covered Pudgy up, I stood there watching Heather run her child like fingers through Pudgy's mane. I asked God, why at such a time did He let it rain. This gave me a sense of urgency to get back into the house and make those phone calls. After a few phone calls I was able to find two men available to come out to the house. God bless these two men, they were so kind, and they deeply felt our sorrow. It did not take long for them to get to the house. I had mentioned to them that my husband was working out of state. I don't think I even had to ask them if they would put Pudge in his grave, they were just kind enough to do so. After they buried him and they had pulled their Bobcat out of the field Heather laid on Pudgy's grave. It was awful. It felt like a curtain had fallen and it was all over.

I went over to their trailer to pay and thank them. They told me they understood. One of the men with tears in his eyes said, he had a dog that was "sure man's best friend". Something happened and he himself had to put it out of its misery. He said it was very devastating to do so. The other man said he had a good dog and he had gone through it too. At the end of this conversation I found out why God made it rain. The two men told me that usually at that time of year they would have been too busy to come out for that type of job. They had been working

20

on a job and got held up by the rain and that was the only reason they were able to come out. They were just hanging around waiting for the rain to stop so they could get back to work; they were also very kind on their price. (Heavenly Father please help those two men many times over). Heather stayed out on Pudgy's grave for a long time.

Some of Pudgy's belongings are kept in Heather's room along with the blue Adidis sweatshirt. Heather hung Pudge's bridle up on the wall above his English saddle, and what he liked the most, his crop. I can still hear the echoes from early on, Heather's teacher would say, "Crop him, crop him Heather; make him listen to you". Pudgy was just playing with Heather, and sometimes he was playing with the teacher. I remember one time I had to leave during one of Heather's lessons although my husband was at home and he and Heather saw the whole thing. Well, Pudge was not listening to Heather, so her teacher decided to get on him and make him listen. Now I had ridden Pudge myself just for fun and I'll tell you, to an adult he was like trying to ride a Popsicle stick. Well, God bless her, she got on Pudge and demanded him to canter. I guess he started to and then, before she knew it, she went sliding down his neck.

Heather and Pudge.

Yes, Pudgy liked to play sometimes, but I believe Pudgy really knew what God wanted him to do. God sent Pudgy to teach Heather to have confidence in herself. I did not know it at the time, but thinking back I can see that I never needed to worry about Heather getting hurt with Pudge. God was also using Pudgy to teach me to have confidence in His providential hand.

THE FIRST NIGHT WITHOUT PUDGE

THE FIRST NIGHT without Pudge, my child suffered! Heather slept in my room that first night and many nights thereafter. She was almost unable to care for herself. She was in agony most of the night. I can not tell you of the heart breaking sound of her cry's of anguish. She would talk in and out of a light sleep. Over and over she would cry, "I want to ride Pudge, my legs! My legs! (She was restless). My legs want to ride Pudgy."

I know all of you avid horsemen can identify with that. It's a feeling you were born with. You ride because you are compelled to.

"Heavenly Father, please bring healing to Heather's broken heart". I had told Heather a true friend will not leave you in great times of need. "Father, only you can look into a man's heart. Father you are a man's only true friend. Amen."

PUDGY IS GONE

PUDGY WAS PUT to sleep the year of 2004. Several months prior to that my husband had taken a job out of state. We had plans to move to the new location but we were unable to find a buyer for our home. My oldest daughter Holly had just graduated and she was ready to leave home, so Heather and I hardly ever saw her. Their absence left Heather and I all alone in the big house which provided a great feeling of loneliness as we were grieving Pudgy's death. The first day I did only what I had to, and Heather did not wake up until early afternoon. What motivated me was knowing that all the other animals were depending on me. As I made my way outside, the dogs' pen is always my first stop and as I climbed over the fence to change their water they did their best to try and cheer me up. They had liked Pudge too. The first year we had Pudge he was the only one of his own kind on the farm; so when he felt he needed some company he would go and stand right by the corner of the dogs' pen. That was Pudgy's special spot and that's where he is buried. He was so cute; He would park himself by backing up into the corner and then stand there with one leg at rest. It must have been a lot of work carrying that pudgy belly around. Pudge was a small pony that could eat like a horse!

Sonny was next in line to be taken care of. I looked down towards the barn and felt hollow inside. I didn't feel like there was much left of me. I had experienced many things in my life but this was not just something that I myself loved, but something that meant the world to my daughter. As I walked toward the barn, a song kept running through my mind. It was a song that I used to sing to Pudge as I would approach the barn. But he wasn't there. All those years I would see his face every morning and now, nothing. I stood at his stall; it smelled of Pudgy. There was his water bucket filled with water and his feed pan filled with food. The baby birds were crying out for their breakfast. I was grieving death and yet there was new life ready to live. It seemed so unfair. I didn't like it but this is the way it must be. We must accept this; it's all for a reason. But some day we'll all see a spring that will never end (all who are in Christ).

Before I took care of Sonny, I sadly opened Pudge's gate, you see, (I always let Pudge out first). I paused so as to let him out and then I closed the gate. I walked Sonny out and before I turned him loose, we stopped at Pudge's grave. Sonny was very quiet and I was crying. I took him a little ways away and turned him loose. He made sure he was far enough away from me before he did something that he had never done before. He let his grief out. He bucked and let out a cry. Throughout the day, I would see Sonny over by Pudge's grave. Now he was alone.

A SMALL BIT OF HAY

I T WAS A small bit of hay that was used to speak to my heart. Jesus used a small bit of spittle at one time to open a blind man's eyes.

Pudge was put to sleep on a Monday. After that sad day Heather was not able to make her way outside until sometime Wednesday morning. Until that morning she had only been out of bed a few times. She would get up and sit quietly in front of the television for an hour or so and then return to bed. There was however, one small interruption. One of our good and dear friends came to our home the next day to quietly sit with us and share our sorrow. Our friend counts the same number of years as does my husband. She is no stranger to a horse barn. She has a good heart and is a true friend. Our friendship is unique. The best way I can think to describe it is this. When my daughter Holly was young she used to like the frog and toad videos. I enjoyed watching them too. For those of you who have never had the pleasure of watching frog and toad, I'll tell you this, it is a friendship of simple pleasure. Frog and toad are two friends that live in a simplistic world and just accept each other as they are. What is seen in the friendship between frog and toad is a very relaxing, old time way. My friends Tuesday visit was very much appreciated and it was at her departure the quiet loneliness returned.

Wednesday morning I went out to the barn to take care of Sonny and clean his stall. It was a nice morning. After that Monday it had been warm and sunny, but very quiet. A ghost town would describe it. It was only Heather and I in that big house. Shortly after my family and I moved here to Central Ohio it was like a whole new world had begun for us. Each one of us seemed to be just fulfilled with the new experience. I remember returning home one day from the store, Heather

25

was with me and as we returned we drove by the front of the house. She was so happy, she said "Oh mom, I love it here, can we live here forever?" Heather was in second grade then. Heather seemed to always have a unique love for her family and friends, always happy and content. It was evident that God had blessed her for that, in the way of her new home and new friends. But now this wonderful world had collapsed and fallen to the ground.

Since that day in which Pudge had gone to sleep I had gone out to the barn everyday to take care of Sonny. And that Tuesday, I remember so clearly asking God - "Do you have Pudge – does he still exist? Please let me know – I realize the answer could be no! - But please give me a sign, something to let me know. Is Pudge with you?" I shared this prayer with Heather. She knew I was hoping for a sign.

Wednesday morning as I was out cleaning Sonny's stall, I happened to notice Heather enter into Pudgy's stall as if she was nothing more than just a whisper. She was pale and the devastation was evident and she seemed to just float about. We were both very sad and didn't say much. At that time we were using straw for bedding in the stalls, there were two whole bales still bound up in his stall, Heather sat down on one of them for awhile. The floor of his stall had a fairly deep layer of straw; it was soft and must have felt good on Heather's bare feet. Heather got up and started to meander about the stall. Due to her pony's age, Pudge would chew on the hay and straw and then let it fall out of his mouth, as if he was unable to chew and than swallow his food a good part of the time. There were always many of these spit wads laying about his stall. He had been doing this for the last few years.

All of a sudden in a soft, quiet voice Heather said to me, "Mom, look." I watched her as she bent down to pick something up. She held in her hand one of the spit wads, she was quite bewildered as she said "Mom, it's still wet." I paused a moment and then reached over through the gate; I took it from Heather and held it in my hand, and sure enough, this one was chewed not long ago. It had to have been chewed shortly before we came out. As I held it in my hand, I looked at Heather and said, "Heather, this must be the sign, the sign I asked for." I went over into Pudge's stall. We were both a little stunned. How could that wadded up straw and hay be so moist? It really was wet enough to have been fairly new. I bent down and started feeling the floor of the stall. The floor of that stall was bone dry. Pudge had gone to sleep late Monday morning and it was now Wednesday. His stall had been empty ever since. Heather had found it by the gate that separated the two stalls next to Sonny. That's where Pudge usually stood. It was just lying on top of the straw. I told Heather that the only thing I could make of it was that it was from God. I told her that probably no one would believe us. I said to Heather, "We're the only ones to witness this". We took the wad into the house and placed it in a glass box where it still remains. A lot of you may think I am just plain silly but, I think there are also some of you who will just smile because you yourselves know how much God loves His children. As for me, I believe that before Pudge had fallen to the ground, (just as Balaams donkey saw an angel) Pudge saw something wonderful.

HOME SWEET HOME

I'M STANDING AT the kitchen window looking at the field that was home to Pudge. Pudge loved his field and his home. It's mid-April and the dandelions are in full-bloom. As I watch the sun sweep across the field of yellow, as it breaks through the clouds, I remember Pudge. I remember his first spring here. We had never had an animal that grazed; Heather and I were so tickled when we had gone out to call Pudge in. He came waddling up to us with a belly full of green grass and a bright yellow nose. We did not know the yellow would rub off. The Spring always brought happiness to Pudge. He sure loved dandelions. I believe Heather had just turned eight and I'm sure you know how eight-year-old girls love to pick flowers. Heather use to fill his feed pan with dandelions, then she would give it to him in his stall and he would eat all to the last dandelion.

As the sun glides across the field highlighting
the yellow as it goes, I can
feel the tears gently slide down my face. It was one of those days where
Jehovah uses the sun and the clouds to highlight the
beautiful things of the earth.
I miss you, Pudgy.

THE FIRST SPRING
WITHOUT PUDGE

ONE SPRING MORNING on one of my trips out to the barn, I was once more reminded of Pudge. There was the blueberry bush. Late April has brought its leaves out again. That was another thing that seemed so out of place. We planted a blueberry bush last spring and we were told that it would not bear fruit until the following year, but it did bear fruit. Heather and I planted two blueberry bushes early that spring and by June one had three berries on it. Heather kept a close eye on the three berries because she did not want the birds to eat them. She wanted to give them to Pudge. But they ripened just a few days too late. Pudge had already gone to sleep. It makes me sad to look at the bush because Heather was so excited about giving the berries to him.

AND THE BABY BIRDS

AND THEN THERE were the baby birds. Pudge was not the only creature in his stall awaiting breakfast. His stall was a home for a nest of baby birds. It seemed so unfair. It seemed to me that Pudge should have gone to sleep after the nesting babies had flown away. It was about a week later they took flight, which made me feel sad. The next few weeks they hung around nearby fluttering in and out of the barn together. The first time I mowed the field without Pudge the young birds came and fluttered about me. I started to cry. I felt it was God trying to tell me that He had not abandoned me in my loneliness. That day they flew away and I never saw them again.

A SLEEPY SURPRISE

I WAS WORN out from traveling and my sleep was restless. It was time to get up but I laid there and prayed "Oh Lord please put me back to sleep for just one more hour". Before I knew it I was ever so gently waking up out of a wonderful dream filled sleep. It was one of those dreams that you can remember the touch and the feel. It was real in that time of slumber. When my mind came to a state of consciousness and knew the dream, I said "Oh thank you Lord". You see not often, but sometimes, He lets the little red pony be real to me again. In my dream I had gone out to the barn and Pudgy was standing there with his little blue halter on. His back was not swayed anymore. I went up to him and I said, "Now you be a good little boy, Pudgy" and he let me feel his whiskers. Sonny was there so I called to him, "Hey Sonny, look who is here," and he came and got to be with his friend.

LORD SET US FREE!

AS I AWOKE one morning, I realized I was dreaming it was still yesterday. Yesterday was a beautiful day, a glorious taste of spring! It was so wonderful my mind did not want to let go; so this was the dream.

I was looking out the window at the day when I saw them. Heather and Sonny (the horse spoken of at the first part of the book) were out playing in the field. They seemed to be having a happy peaceful time. One was just as happy as the other. They had each other and that was all that mattered (God given contentment!). All of a sudden they were up by the window. With an expression of a likeness of myself, Heather glanced at me and smiled, nodded her head as if to let me know. It happened! I have been freed! My chains are gone. Heather's soul had been set free. God set forth a rhythm and it was placed before Heather and her God given horse to follow, and they rode forth.

After I awoke and remembered the dream, I quickly tried to go back to sleep. I have waited so long to see that freedom in Heather's face and it was only a dream. But I believe it was hope sent from God!

HEAVENLY FATHER, PLEASE MAKE MORE LITTLE RED PONIES!

I MYSELF HAD a little red pony, the only problem was that six hundred miles were between us. My family lived in a small city in the North. I was born in Gary, Indiana. My grandparents lived way down south in the country and we would go once or twice a year to visit them. Those visits could never come soon enough for me. I loved my grandparents and their home in Tennessee. Deep in my heart, that would be where I felt at home. I always wanted, more than anything, to live with them. It was such a different world than the one I lived in. I loved the south and the people there. I admired their ways and often imagined what it would be like to be a part of that world. My grandparents are in heaven now. I hope when I get there, the Lord will have a place tucked away, fixed just like the South. I also would like to think that God will let me stay there with my grandparents and know what it would have been like to live with them in the South.

My grandpa was a pretty strict old man. He wasn't shy about listing your sins. I did not always like to hear it, but that was okay because I loved him so much. My grandpa was one of a kind and I thank God that he had the courage to tell me. He loved me! I needed to know wrong from right. I sure will be glad to see him again. I think he died not knowing that I had made it (God has taken my soul). I know he had prayed a lot of prayers for me. We never talked much, but I always had this feeling that he believed in me.

One of the things I admired about my grandpa was he never forgot to say grace before each meal. They always conducted themselves in a very proper manner. My grandma, "God bless her", would fix a good meal, set the table and never put a place for herself. With my grandma gracefully standing off to the side we all would sit down. My grandpa would always be at the head of the table and no one was to touch a thing until someone had said grace. My sweet grandma would stand politely by the table and bow her head. After grace was said, she would then go to waiting on everybody. My grandma would always wait until everyone had finished eating and gotten up and gone before she would sit herself down and eat. She honored God by serving others.

My grandparents knew that my childhood dream was to have a horse. My grandpa would get after my dad sometimes; he would say "Waymon" you ought to move down here so Susan can have herself a horse". By the time I and reached about the age of fourteen my grandpa had gotten tired of waiting. One day we all got some unexpected news. My grandpa called to tell my dad to bring Susan to Tennessee; he had bought her a pony. It was an old plow pony and they thought it had been broke to ride. After the call, a trip to Tennessee was then planned. I was so taken back by the fact that someone had actually bought a pony just for me that I really did not know what to think. They were poor in the way in which nothing gets misused. I remember my grandma carefully keeping her hair pins so as not to lose one. This was strange to me and I did not know why. Their frugalness was so unique to me and I loved them so much, I used to ask God if I could live just the way my grandma did. Later on in my life, He was kind enough to do so and I learned of how they suffered. But that is when you learn to trust God to provide. Hard times will lead you to a straight and narrow path.

The relationship between my grandpa and me was somewhat like what was seen in the good old movie (Heidi). The relationship in the beginning of the movie between Heidi and her grandfather is a good portrait of mine with my grandpa. Heidi's grandfather came across as being cold towards the world. I did not know it then but I do know it now, that my grandpa loved me very much.

The pony's name was Dolly and the first time I saw Dolly I still did not quite know what to think. My sister and I would take turns riding.

She liked Tennessee too and we had many adventures there. Later I found out that my grandma got enjoyment from watching us out of her kitchen window.

One day after I had finished riding Dolly I had gone into the kitchen. That is usually where you could find my grandma; she told me that she had been watching me ride. I don't believe that up until then, anyone really knew how these poor old folks came up with the money to buy old Dolly; And that day I found out. She told me that my grandpa had cut some of their trees, and had cut and hewed them all by hand. She told me how much work it was for him at his age and how work like that had really taken its toll on him. He cut just enough to earn forty dollars, which was the price of Dolly. I believe she wanted me to know my grandpa cared very much for me.

THE SHEPHERD!

ALL THROUGH MY childhood years as well as my young adult life I believed that I was saved by Jesus, but there was always a distance, deep down inside. I knew I wasn't good enough for Him. There was a wall in which I saw no gate.

The day came, and when it was the Lord's time, this wall of distance was melted away. One day in my search to become closer to God I came across a Keith Green cassette tape (Keith Green – *Songs for the Shepherd*). The first time I heard his voice a feeling came about that is impossible to describe. It was like for the first time I really knew what true love is. I knew how it felt to love your parents, husband, children, sisters, and so on. And I very much remember my single life and all those times I thought I had found my true love! But this was different than all those types of feelings. This love was not the kind of love that is found here in this world. It's not a feeling of "I have special feelings for someone and need that person to also have the same feelings for me". This was a feeling of knowing something other than myself, yet this love satisfied me to the core of my being. What I heard in Keith Green's voice was the love of Jesus. This sound of love brought forth tears that just dripped from my eyes. I listened to this tape for many months and when the tears had melted down the wall of distance I did not need to search for love anymore. There was a new place beyond that wall.

I also stumbled across the book about Keith Green's life. I was amazed by his love for Jesus and the journey he had made to find Him. As I learned more about him through his songs and book, I learned that he so wanted to be like Jesus by sharing his joy with those who knew no joy, and share his laughter with those who had forgotten how to laugh.

He, too, was a shepherd.

February 3, 2013

THE FIRST CALL

(From a mouth to an ear to a heart)

ONE PARTICULAR SUNDAY, not so very long ago, the pastor
of our church dismissed us be saying, "Go and be like Jesus to
someone today". From a mouth to an ear to a heart the mission was
sent. The pastor's commissioned words lay in my ears. My husband and
I then decided to return home and there spent a quiet Sunday. As the
day played out, among my husband, daughter and I, we spent a peaceful
day with not much interaction.

Slowly time gave change to the day and as night put the daylight
to sleep, my mind began to engage thoughts of slumber. My heart sank
low. The commission was still in my ears. Feeling a little down I decided
to get behind a closed door to do some reading and spend some quite
time with God. There at my desk lay my Bible, containing the bulletin
for that Sunday. Our bulletin always contains a *Good News Daily* insert
with a reading for each day of the week. As I opened my Bible and
began to read, a soft soothing thought entered my mind. Two weeks
had gone by since my last telephone conversation with my sister. Her
only son, at the age of 29, passed away almost one year ago. Ah ha, she
may be the one!

I reached for the telephone feeling that Jesus was right there with
me. As the telephone rang, I focused on the bulletin insert. When my
sister answered the phone she was crying. She had also been spending
time with God. I asked her if I could read something to her from
the *Good News Daily* bulletin insert. She said "Yes, please". Since the

day was Sunday I decided to go with the reading for the day. When I finished the reading she cried all the more. She said, "Oh, how did you know? That's just what I had been talking to God about." She said, "I was pleading with God to give me an answer to my questions and now the phone rang and it is you with a reading that brings answers pertaining to my questions". She said again; "Sue how did you know." I said "I did not know". I told her it was not me, it was God. He knows. All I did was to try and follow the instructions.

My testimony is this:
I must go to church and listen. Now I'm
afraid to miss a Sunday service.
Praise be to God.

THE SECOND CALL

(From a hand to a mouth to an ear.)

ON SUNDAY, FEBRUARY 24th I went to church to attend the new members class. There I was given a small booklet titled "Why Jesus"? Again I did as previous to my last testimony. On a Sunday evening I sat down to spend time with God and study his word. I gathered my Bible and an assortment of writings to read. Since I had attended the new members class earlier that day I thought it would be good to look at the readings I had received. First I read the little booklet called "Why Jesus"? The reading on page 11 was titled "Why did He come to earth?" The reading was short, direct and informative. The writer was not shy about explaining the pain Christ endured for the sinner. After reading about why and how Jesus was crucified, I set the booklet down. After a long pause to honor Christ, my sister once again came to mind; and once again I felt the stage was set to call her, so I did. When she answered the phone, she was angry and crying. She had now come to the hard side of the grieving process. Anger can be a person's worst enemy. She told me that just a short time before I called her, she had asked her husband to leave the room because she now felt angry at God. "She said why did God take my son? Why did He take my son away from me?" I offered to hang up the phone if she needed me to. I was glad when she said no, and at that moment, in my heart, I praised God for what I received at church that very day. I felt so blessed to be at His work for, as I had mentioned above, I had just finished reading the small booklet the pastor had given me.

I asked her so carefully if I could read something to her. She said "sure". I read to her the reading on page11. After reminding her of the explanation on the crucifixion of Christ, I told her that if her son had been the only one among all men to be saved, Christ would still have come to give himself as a ransom. Now, she took a long pause and the sound of her cry changed from bitter to great sadness. Jesus' work on the cross brought a change to her heart.

She now said to me "Oh Sue, I feel so embarrassed. I'm so ashamed. I should have never been thinking like I was. It is so hard. I'm so sorry." I saw God work through his body of people, the body of Christ.

From a hand to a mouth to an ear; His
love went into a woman's heart.
My testimony:
I am so glad I went to the new members class. I
am so glad I have him watching over me.
Praise be to God.
- In remembrance of Billy Holtzman -

A TRIBUTE TO ENRIQUE GARCIA

A dear friend

I HAVE NEVER known a man so dedicated to his wife and daughters such as Enrique Garcia. He honored Gods institute for the family. His honor for the institute of family overflowed on to our family: This we will cherish until we see him again.

Our family came to Ohio in 1998. We did not have one relative in the state. Enrique came to Ohio in 2008. Right at the onset Enrique became family to us. Shortly there after he brought his family to Ohio and they all together were a blessing. Enrique's person-hood there in Ohio gave us family. Like family should be, he was always someone there ready to talk with and spend time with us.

Enrique enjoyed providing for his family. It was so frequently spoken of. I can't help but think that it was one of the highest's callings in his mind. On many occasions he told us he also had provided for his family for a time when he would be gone from their presence.

You can never have enough time with loved one's here on earth. Enrique always made it a priority to spend time with friends and family. Enrique knew the value of life! So I ask all to give great consideration to this value Enrique held so high.

Enrique was a leader: Leaders do not forget to laugh. At every get together we had with Enrique he made sure everyone was spoken too and made sure humor was offered to all.

Enrique spoke hope to all of his days and invited others to do the same. He was a inspiration. He was a man that knew how to put hope into each and every step he took. The last three years each step was a mountain climb. There were many occasions Enrique asked me to pray for him. More than once I believe his heart made a confession of faith. With that said I believe he is now at the top of that mountain.

From what I saw Enrique Garcia lived by the rules of Providence: He loved his wife and kept his daughters from going astray!

Enrique took his last step with honor.

A PEPPERED HAM!

MY FAMILY AND I moved to North Central Ohio from Northern Indiana during the month of August 1998; it was there and then we purchased a new home. When we sold our house in Indiana we still had some property and buildings that had not yet sold. We decided to purchase our new home without the buildings and land being sold. My husband and I had always tried to live within our means. The first year in our new home was a year of learning to become as frugal as one can. Four years prior to this move; when I was about thirty three years old my husband and I made the decision that I would quit my job and stay at home to care for our two daughters, Holly and Heather.

In preparation for the first Christmas in our new home I did a lot of talking to God. I needed to be frugal and that meant even being frugal with the Christmas dinner. I remember planning the dinner before I went shopping. I was going to make a fairly inexpensive sausage, Swiss cheese, and sauerkraut dish for the main course. Before I went to the meat market I remember talking to God, and I know better than to make promises to Him! But I asked Him to help me to only spend what I could afford and I would try my very best to get only what was on my list. Whenever you have a conversation like that with God, expect to be enticed. As I made my way through the store collecting only the items written on the list I was happy and doing great. I was so content because I was following my list, but after telling the butcher how much sausage I would like to have, my eyes started to wander. There in the glass case was a beautiful peppered ham. Temptation set in! This time it seemed like it took the butcher an extra long time to get my sausage packaged. I had a good long look at that peppered ham. Oh, how my two girls would love some nice, big chunk's of ham for Christmas dinner. After leaving the meat market I cannot tell you how many times I thought about that peppered ham. I stuck to it though, I was determined that if God did not give me the money to purchase that ham I was just not supposed to have it. However there were many times I found myself trying to figure out some way I could go back and get it. My girls had grown up in such a frugal home and I so desired to prepare and serve a Christmas meal fitting for the beautiful new home that God had been so generous with.

Well, I had made it! With just a day or two before Christmas and no more cash at hand I had passed the test, the peppered ham would have to wait until next Christmas. BUT GOD WAS WATCHING! And, on the twenty third of December my husband and I had gone to bed as we usually do about ten o'clock at night. Not long after my husband had turned out the light something strange happened, there was a knock at the front door. My husband and I froze. How strange, we were still fairly new to the area and certainly did not think that we had yet known anyone well enough to receive a visitor that late at night. My husband quickly got up, turned the light on and got dressed. We were both sleepy-eyed and wondering who this mysterious visitor could be. I quietly waited as I heard my husband make his way down the stairs and opened the front door. I heard the voices of two men. I listened as the door closed and my husband made his way back up the stairs carrying a large box. He explained to me that the man at the door was the Realtor that sold us our home. He told my husband this year his agency had decided to thank the people who purchased homes through their agency that year by giving a gift at Christmas time. He sat down on the bed and then opened the box. He was silent and intently stared at what was inside. This strange event had set the stage for my imagination to run wild. I asked, "What is it"? And he said, "It's a ham". "A hand"? I said! "No, it's a ham," He replied. It was a peppered Ham! A great big peppered ham just like the one I saw at the butcher shop. When I realized what was going on, I knew. I knew that there was only one way that could have happened.

What do you think?

Mo on Sonny's Back

MO THE SUITCASE

HOW CLEVER HEATHER is, really! Who would ever think of turning a goat into a suitcase? We have a little pygmy goat whose name is Mo, and as she grew she became quite heavy. She was always getting out of her pen. Goats do not always willingly follow along and it got to be quite a struggle to carry her if she would refuse to return to her pen by the use of her own four legs. So Heather took an old horse halter and tailored it to fit so she could put it on the little goat and pick her up and carry her just like a suitcase. It even had a handle on top. With a little ingenuity, Mo was transformed into a furry black suitcase with four legs. This easy to carry suitcase gave birth to an even more advanced idea. So once more I was called out to the barn. Heather stood there pleased as she could be with herself and said, "Hey, look! I have put Mo up in the hay loft". With the understanding in mind that there is no ladder going up to the hay loft, with a burst of laughter I said, "How in the world did you get Mo up there"? Well I must say, as she began to show me, I was just as pleased with her as she was. She had her thinking cap on! Heather rigged up a pulley system from a roof rafter and with Mo dressed in her suit case attire she hoisted her little friend up. Oh! Don't worry, Mo was quite safe. Actually I think Mo had a lot of fun. That's one of the cute things about goats. They always have a happy smile on their face and quite the simple mind to go along with it.

A DARK SURPRISE

I REMEMBER WHEN my older sister and I were young, we loved to play hide and go seek, although it was more exciting when my dad would join us. I remember one specific evening when my dad turned all the lights in the house off, with the exception of the television and one lamp in the living room where my mother was. I remember our anticipation as we waited for him to say "Ready". My sister and I would then go and find him. I remember as we played in the darkened house that it was fun for awhile, but my sister and I began to need a little more excitement. We wanted it darker so we talked my mom into letting us turn off the light in the living room, we even wanted her to turn off the television but she thought that was going too far. (My dad gets a big kick out of teasing my mom for being afraid of the dark!) Well, we got it as dark as we could and our excitement was high and, with my sister holding me in front of her, I remember us slowly making our way down the hall. There is almost a four year difference between my sister and me. I guess she thought she could endure the shock of my dad jumping out of the darkness better with me standing in front of her. Every time we came to a place where she thought my dad might be, she would push me towards that place. If nothing happened, she would hold me in front of her again and quietly move on. Now we finally came to a corner of a room where she had this eerie feeling. I remember her whispering "I think there's something there". She was scared with excitement. As it happened, I received the first of the two unexpected surprises. Without notice, my father's hand came through the darkness and took me. I remember him pulling me close to him and putting his hand to my mouth as to not say a word.

Imagine the surprise she got! It was quite the opposite of what was anticipated; instead of a loud, sudden scare, she received the quiet dark scare of nothing! It was the scare of being alone in the dark.

It's of great comfort to know that someday, God the Father My Creator, is going to, without notice, reach out His hand and take me into safety.

AT THE FAIR

A S I STEPPED onto the cart of a buck board as it had just began to move I was lunged forward yet at the same time thrashed backward. The door to my youth was jarred open as my physical body gracefully remembered to adapt and balance; my mind was taken back to long ago days in Tennessee. Southern Sisters of a past time they were. There I was received and there, in their contentment did I abide. It was at one of the four crossroads my Father seldom ever traveled. But not a stranger to the way.

The regenerate soul, moves about, indwelt, by Him, who is past present and future for all time. It is He who gives us the ability to remember the past while being in the present. I think that is a remarkable lend-ed attribute.

Thank You Father for Your kindness!

THE BIRDS WEAR PINK!

A FRIEND INVITED me to a bible study he was heading up and was hoping for a good turnout. I was determined to go because I had noticed what a kind person he was to all. I was running late due to the reluctance I was feeling. I had never been to that church before and knew but one person. My husband and I attended a Vineyard Church which is quite casual. The one I was going to visit, dates back somewhere to the 1840's and it was, to my knowledge, a more conservative dress. I was worried about what to wear. I should have left fifteen minutes ago, but with wet hair and changing my outfit for the third time I said to myself, "Hey, you're just going to have to go!"

I was worried that the bright flamingo pink Capris I had on were going to be too... Much! But they looked nice. The rich color had such an up lifting effect. I jumped in the car and away I went. I was still dissatisfied with what I was wearing but I did not want to disappoint my Father and as I made my way up to the steps of His house He gave me a desire to go in. My friend met me at the door and as he ushered me into the room I saw, to the delight of my eyes, a woman who greeted me with her hand held out. With a soft friendly smile she said "Hi! I am Pastor Sharon". She was so beautiful as she stood there wearing almost the same cut pattern of Capris and what do you think? Almost the same exact shade of flamingo pink!

IT'S TIME TO REFRESH THE ROOM!

I painted a room.
I hung a mirror and saw what was not seen before.
There in the mirror was the window. There
in the window was a new house.
I did a double take.
No, I have not seen it before.
How is that so?
The other house is still there
It was in plain view through the window just moments ago.
It's the mirror!
Its something I don't know!
I like this mirror. It is in a good place!
What I see in the mirror makes me feel new and clean.

1 CORINTHIANS 13: 11-13 It's like this: when I was a child I spoke and thought and reasoned as a child does. But when I became a man my thoughts grew far beyond those of my childhood, and now I have put away the childish things. 12 In the same way, we can see and understand only a little about God now, as if we were peering at his reflection in a poor mirror; but someday we are going to see him in his completeness, face to face. Now all that I know is hazy and blurred, but then I will see everything clearly, just as clearly as God sees into my heart right now.

13 There are three things that remain: faith, hope, and love- and the greatest of these is love.

Foot Note: When viewed from different angles; life and objects change our view and perception.

THE WINDOW

Beside my window is where I sat.
Upward there-of I took a glance.
A droplet of water was intent on my eye.
A thought came about:
Does God know?
Does God know that this small droplet of water
is hanging from the gutter of my house?
Then it was as clear as the droplet itself...
He knows!
He knows because I'm looking at it
as He abides within!
I watched as the unseen wind intermingled
with the droplet changing it's
form many times over.
All of a sudden the wind had brought such
change of form to the droplet that the wind
had now picked it up and carried it away.

Father, hold me forever in your arms.
Amen

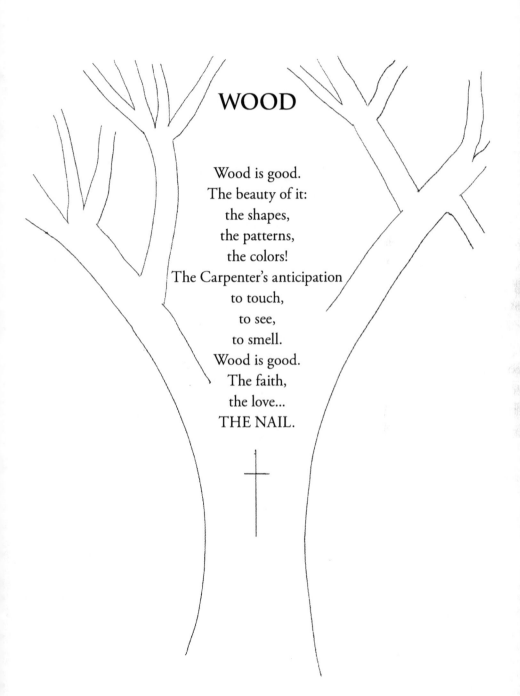

WOOD

Wood is good.
The beauty of it:
the shapes,
the patterns,
the colors!
The Carpenter's anticipation
to touch,
to see,
to smell.
Wood is good.
The faith,
the love...
THE NAIL.

DEAR NEIGHBOR, MY FRIEND

Time has grown up around us.
The earth, the trees.
The open is closed.
The across the way holler is stilled...
Thus
A new life of silent conversation moves on ahead of us.
But now...
Still here...
Still there.
The enjoyment of the friendship in a smile,
The comfort found in the wave of a hand.
As neighbors let us share together the soft fall of the leaves.
Let the laughter of the earth be our words to one another.
May He bless the hearts of friendship to
expand into more than just time.

MY BOY NOAH

You remembered,
The entrance - the smell - the sound – the place.
Quiet...
And there I stood!
Waiting – hoping - wanting – loving.
Then in a moments rest,
Providence unveiled and blessed.
You approached so quietly as if moved in by His hand.
Your little arms gently hold so tight
Not a word spoken just the remembrance.
Your familiar face buried into my heart fell upon my stature;
Grandma - I remember
It's Me, your boy Noah!

THE ROD

And as a man's hand
reaches out to catch
a heavy rod,
so doth
you oh Lord,
catch my heart as a weighted
stone;
Turn it white
and write my Name
as it is,
and will be
unknown.

REVELATION 2:17 "LET everyone who can hear, listen to what the Spirit is saying to the churches: Every one who is victorious shall eat of the hidden manna, the secret nourishment from heaven; and I will give to each a white stone, and on the stone will be engraved a new name that no one else knows except the one receiving it.

Psalm 23: 4 (ESV) Even though I walk through the valley of the shadow of death, I will fear no evil. For you are with me; your rod and your staff, they comfort me.

HONEY

The sweet cream of honey
melts out from the heart of love.
O faith, move into my heart
and know my Soul.

Go into my Spirit and Thy
salvation deliver.

Spring upward the Joy of my Soul!
With the sweet cream of honey
faithfully go.

GOD LIGHTS THE WORLD

THE VAPOR CRYSTALS dance in the air like outdoor dust particles, each one reflecting the marvel of God. Trillions of miniature rays floating right in front of my eyes. All I can do is stand there. I am held at rest by my Creator. He sends His light therapy to be enjoyed even in the winter. I stand silent and admire God for His work. I forget the cold as trillions of crystals dazzle my eyes; just as beautiful as diamonds, reflecting all the colors of the rainbow, and the cost is nothing, free to anyone who will pause for a moment and notice. Upon the sunrise I have been greatly blessed!

Before the Lord opened my eyes these few words were not fully heard or understood. The Bible tells us; "This bowl of wrath can be found simmering in the heart of mankind". Warning! The following ingredients may lead to death".

WICKED SOUP

Narcissism
Envy
Favoritism

And does not favoritism walk so smoothly with narcissism? Favoritism says to narcissism, "I like only you because I like only what I like," and envy stirs the pot.

Endorsed
By
Treason

PEOPLE

People don't always do things on purpose.
Sometimes they just don't understand.
But sometimes they do!
I should do well to remember...
Only He knows the difference!

HOPE

"O" Lord, please help me to walk peacefully down the
path you have chosen for me.
And, "O" Lord, may your kindness flow out to me when my inner
being is deceived and weak.
But "O" Lord, forgive me most when I myself
have deceived my own mind.
For this would be when I am furthest from thee.
Teach me, to let things happen according to you!

We forfeit happiness when we demand our own way!
Demanding our own way is to put demands on God!

One of the best memories I have of Heather's childhood is this:
To My Heather
From your
Sweet Mommy

Very often throughout our days Heather would say to me in a cute little sing song way, "My sweet Mommy". When I heard her sing this I knew to brace myself because usually this little tune was followed up with a great big bear hug. It was our little game; I would always sing back to her, "My sweet Heather"! A little expression of love can bless a heart in a big bear hug of a way!

When I would pick Heather up from a friend's house or school she would always be glad to see me. The first glance of me would stop her from whatever she was doing. On looking mothers were usually a bit taken back from the greeting I would receive. Heather would always race towards me to give me a big bear hug! The older she got the bigger the hug. There were a few times she almost knocked me off my feet!

STEP BY STEP

It's a funny thing: I used to be one way and then the other.
He makes me strong and then He makes me weak.
He puts the shoe on one foot and then the other.
When I am weak, I pray "Oh Lord, make me strong.
Then He says to me, "Don't you see?!"
The strong and the weak are to walk hand in hand.

WATER

LORD, HELP ME to not be affected by the movement of different waters. You have given me a stream of life to follow and follow I must. The stream is smooth and peaceful while moved by your flow. Intermingled with different waters my stream is moved and pushed out of place. As the stream inside seeps out to find its way, thus, the current will guide the flow. May that of your spirit be thus that flows out unto me.

PERSONAL PRAYERS

Father may your good news shine in our eyes and may those
who see it remember the work and sacrifice of Christ.

Jesus,
As you walked the earth the one who sought your
life seeks to silence the lives of your people.
Comfort us with your safe keeping.

Father I pray for crystal clear forgiveness, joy and peace.
For we are your creation,
and belong to you alone.
Please, Father summon us unto your Throne.

Jesus said I will never leave you or forsake you!
This is true
This is so true.
This is the truth!

BE STILL AND KNOW
THAT I AM GOD!

Aa ha... The storm is gone.
Left behind is a gentle rain.
The movement of the wind stands quiet.
I watch as the rain falls straight down.
Father I like this rain. This straight
falling down rain is so personable. You send
each rain drop straight down
from Heaven right atop onto me.
Soaked as I am the sun burst
forth and fills my eyes.
Glory be to God
in the highest!

Father, I feel like fragile glass that will shatter as the wind blows.

Printed in the United States
By Bookmasters